Howard Duffield

A Noble Life

Howard Duffield

A Noble Life

ISBN/EAN: 9783337780081

Printed in Europe, USA, Canada, Australia, Japan

Cover: Foto ©Thomas Meinert / pixelio.de

More available books at **www.hansebooks.com**

BY

HOWARD DUFFIELD, D.D.,

MINISTER OF THE FIRST PRESBYTERIAN CHURCH,
NEW YORK CITY.

NEW YORK:

ANSON D. F. RANDOLPH & COMPANY,

(INCORPORATED)

182 FIFTH AVENUE.

The Love of Christ constraineth us.

2 CORINTHIANS iv. 14.

A NOBLE LIFE.

COMMONPLACE chafes. Humdrum galls. Monotony grinds. Yet they are our inseparable companions. They keep step with us the whole of the way. We are never far from their side, never out of their sight. No wonder that sometimes the clouds hang low, and heaven is hidden. No wonder that heart failure is frequent. No wonder that the moment comes when living seems drudging ; when we tire of trying ; when even in this high noon of modern knowledge we stand tongue-tied before the stony challenge of the ancient sphinx :—

"What of it all, when it all is done?"

From the deep places of the human heart there rises a hungry cry for greatness. Weariedly we reach out "lame hands," if haply we may but touch the hem of majesty. With unsleeping eyes we peer into every quarter for a glimpse of grandeur. We persist in looking the wrong way. We keep on beating the wrong bush. The sublimity which we seek is not without us, but within.

The man wants manhood who can gaze unthrilled upon the spires and domes of the cathedral-like mountains, or walk unstirred the pillared

aisles of forest temples ; or listen un-
awed to the weird and never quiet
diapason of the sea. The man is
lacking in finest faculty who is not
enkindled by the majestic ideas
which have been chiselled into
stately marbles, or pencilled upon
the glowing canvas ; who is not en-
thralled by the matchless harmonies
through which master spirits have
whispered their mysterious secrets to
uncounted generations ; who is not
enchanted by the spell of the pen, that
magic wand with which the magicians
of the mind, shape the course of the
world. But more sublime than
sculptured stone, or snow-crowned
Alps, or sweetest music, or richest
rhetoric, is a noble life. Character

dwarfs the most magnificent of things inanimate. Soul is the true patent of nobility. Royalty of spirit may be uninvested with the circumstances of external grandeur. The noble heart may look out upon the world through a face that is homely. It may move upon a plane that is lowly. It may spend its energies upon endeavors that are ordinary. Its possessor may be "in bodily presence weak, and in speech contemptible," but let head and hand and heart be welded in the furnace glow of a lofty and uplifting purpose, and men recognize the king.

It was intensity of purpose that put power into Paul. There never lived a man so dead in earnest as that little tent-maker from Tarsus. "Deserts beheld him battling with their sand-storms. Fierce river torrents were breasted by his arm. Ocean held him a solitary waif floating upon its surface. Again and again did the cruel sea cast him shipwrecked upon the land, and the land sent him back full of high and holy enterprise to ocean. Singing at midnight in the dungeon, weaving tent-cloth at the loom, disputing among the philosophers upon Mars Hill, marching over the stones of the Appian Way, clanking his fetters while he writes in his hired house in Rome, —where, and in what employ do we not find this strangely fervent man?" Ordinary motives had lost their grip upon him. Trial could not depress him. Toil could not daunt him. These things were his glory. What spark kindled such flaming zeal? What magnetism drew him on and helped him up in the face of such relentless opposition? What talisman, with mystic power, enabled that man to conquer all the foes that challenge the progress of a human soul? Can his secret be mastered by other minds? Can that energy be generated within our hearts? Hearken to his answer: "The love of Christ constraineth us." The simple, single secret of a noble life is the constraining power of a Saviour's love.

There had been a day when Paul

regarded the death of Christ with very different feelings. There had been a day when the thought of the crucifixion only wreathed his lips with a stern smile of satisfaction that a malefactor had suffered his just deserts. There was a day when the single impulse which the death of the Nazarene imparted to the man of Tarsus was the spur of a vindictive frenzy to exterminate His followers. But the light that flooded the Damascus highway with glory, flashed radiance upon Golgotha. Paul discovered that the hill of Calvary was the summit of sublimity; that the thorn crown of Jesus was the diadem of an ineffable royalty; that the cross crimsoned with agony was the altar of a mysterious sacrifice of love, whereon the victim had made an offering of himself. He now caught with quickened hearing those tender accents, "The Son of man has come to seek and to save that which was lost, and to give His life a ransom for many." His soul melted as he listened to the quivering accents of the dying sufferer while He prayed for the forgiveness of His foes. The knowledge of that grace brought Paul to a knowledge of himself. All opposition to the Christ went down before the flood of feeling that came surging out at the touch of a mercy great enough to take him into its embrace. Standing before the cross of Jesus, he loses sight of everything else, and raises the exultant shout, "God forbid that I should glory save in that cross of my Lord Jesus Christ; for He was the Son of God, and He loved, and He died for me."

This feeling of personal interest in the love of the crucified Jesus made it sheer impossibility for that man to live a life of commonplace. He felt the pressure of that motive to be phenomenal. He ransacks his affluent vocabulary to find the phrase that will aptly express its intensity. With vulture-eyed nicety he swoops upon a word used in the New Testament to express all kinds of resistless power: the surge of a crowd, the clutch of the police, the tenacity of disease, and as though the impulse of a noble life generated by personal recognition of the Saviour's love, summed up and exceeded the might exhibited in all these ways, he writes with flaming heart and ardent pen, "The love of Christ constraineth us." That sentence was Paul's biography in brief. The love of Christ constrained him to lay his heart at the foot of the cross. It sustained him under the smitings of adversity. It inflamed him with its summons to arduous and chivalrous service. It restrained him when chafed by the oppositions of brutality and stupidity. It remained with him in the lonely shadow hours of desertion and bereavement. The heart of Jesus was the dynamo that electrified his life. Its energy is no whit wasted. The circuit along which its power travels can still be established. When the negative pole of human need is brought into contact with the positive pole of the grace of Christ, the life is pervaded with the play of those elemental forces which built Paul. Each, in our measure, may be charged with the same ennobling energy.

I. Note the soul-saving power of the "love of Christ." Allusion to the power of Jesus, ordinarily causes the thought to revert to those marvels of His earthly story when He trod the storm-chafed sea as though a pavement of marble was beneath His sandals,—when pain and grief fled before His presence, like spectres at sunrise, when He reversed the irrevocable, and the spirits of the dead hastened at His call to recross the threshold of the tomb. But the conversion of a soul surpasses in display of divine energy those works of wonder recorded upon the pages of the evangelists. Martin Luther weighed every syllable when he wrote, " Regeneration is the greatest of miracles." The pen of inspiration made no slip when it inscribed in the same category, the creation of the universe, the resurrection of the Lord from the dead, and the conversion of the soul. Every time a man is converted there is re-creation and resurrection ; but there is no longer an empty void to be peopled with existences by a fiat of deity ; there is no longer a cold and shrouded body to be awakened from its death sleep by a syllable of power. There is a living soul, saturated and suffused with antagonism to the Almighty. There is a rebel will ; its every energy embattled against the Lord of Hosts. There is a quick and throbbing spirit, pulsing with hostility to Him who sits upon the throne. Omnipotence can break that will ; but the problem is, to bend it. Omnipotence can crush that heart ; but the problem is, to change it. Omnipotence can grind that enemy into powder ; but the problem is, to transform antagonism

17

into allegiance. Can sheer Almightiness ever constrain a single individual to surrender his prejudices; prejudices that have not merely been engrafted by education, but implanted by birth; prejudices that have been cultured into convictions; convictions that have flowered into habits; habits that have fruited into the seemingly necessary laws of being?

Souls cannot be dragooned into holiness. The baton of the policeman cracks the skull, but cannot dent the heart. Hatred is not to be clubbed into love. Guilt may be handcuffed and jailed, but the logic of the patrol wagon and the prison cell does not make a bad man a better man. Siberia makes no allegiance to the Czar. State the problem and it seems insoluble. Jesus solved it. Jesus said, " I, if I be lifted up, will draw all men unto Me." Iron bends to the magnetism of the cross. Adamant melts under the electric currents of the love of Christ. Hearts become willing when they catch the meaning of Jesus' death. Wills become yielding when face to face with the crucified Redeemer. Mercy is stronger than might. Love is more potent than omnipotence. Tenderness is Titanic. The crown of thorns is more imperial than the wreath of laurel. It is the talisman of universal conquest. Saul of Tarsus felt its power. It changed him from a pharisaic persecutor of Christians, into the Napoleon of the early church. Augustine of Carthage felt its power. It transformed the pagan roué into the prince of theological thinkers. Martin Luther felt its power. It emancipated him from bondage to cowled superstition and anointed him as the pioneer champion of human liberty. John Newton felt its power. It raised him from a moral degradation lower than that of the slaves he sold, and it made him a liberator of Satan's captives. John Bunyan felt its power. "Grace Abounding" snatched him as a brand from the burning and made him a guide for pilgrims to the Celestial City. John B. Gough felt its power. It caught him from a gutter grave, and it taught him to sound the bugle-call of a rescue work, the echoes of which reverberate around the globe. Jerry McAuley felt its power. It floated the banners of eternal hope over the black despair of a Water Street dive. The magnetic pole of the world is marked by the socket of the cross. The fountain - head of the most triumphant of energies is the heart that broke on Calvary.

II. Note the character-building power of the "love of Christ." Character to be strong must be con-centrated. Rays of light scattered, warm. Focused, they burn. So the love of Christ by gathering up the straggling beams of man's influence, and centering them upon a single exalted purpose, puts a fervency into life that can be kindled by no other flame. Unrestrained, the brook streams gently across the meadow. Enclosed within the narrow channel of the race, it drives with resistless momentum the powerful mechanism of the mill. So the love of Christ, by cutting a man off from earthly ends, and hemming a man in from selfish aims and shutting a man up to a way that is strait and narrow, but high and holy, causes the entire machinery of his being to move with a power and momentum that is derivable from no other impulse. " The love of Christ " is the precise form of energy for which Plato longed when, heartsick at the moral debasement of his fellow-men, he said that humanity could never be exalted, save by the lever of "loyalty to a divine person." The philosopher diagnosed keenly. All the after centuries have attested the accuracy of his insight. Loyalty to a divine person has pointed the few paragraphs in human history which can be read without a blush or tear. Loyalty to a divine person has cradled and nurtured the choicest spirits of our race: such typical forms of manhood as the princely William of Orange, who battled no less stoutly for the honor of Christ, than he did for the freedom of the down-trodden Netherlands; like the poet-statesman Milton, who devoted that imperial intellect which was the guardian of England's honor, to the unfolding of the ways of God to man; like that intellectual giant, Sir Isaac Newton, whose eagle-eyed intellect scanned with equal interest the marvels of God's works, and the mysteries of God's word; like big-brained Daniel Webster, who in the clear light of his evening time wrote, " Lord, I believe; help Thou my unbelief "; like Bismarck, that man of iron and fire, who said, " If I were not a Christian and a firm believer, you would never have had such a chancellor "; like Gladstone, who not only lays his lance in rest for the maintenance of human rights, but is armored cap-a-pie for the honor of the word of God ; like Kepler and Faraday ; like Herschel and Agassiz, like Clerk Maxwell, and Stanley, and Drummond,—who counted it as their highest achievement to think the thoughts of God after Him, and have made it their loftiest ambition to win the children of God back to Him. Loyalty to a divine Person is the salt-principle of humanity, alone preserving it from entire corruption. Loyalty to a divine Person is the leaven power of the race, alone infusing it with the energies which can achieve its regeneration.

Life is not all achievement. It is endurance ; and to endure is a much harder thing than to act. It is easier to prance than to plod. It is easier for the tongue to slip its leash than to wear its curb. It is easier to strike from the shoulder than to keep the fingers unclenched at the side. It is easier to charge with the bayonet than to trudge with the knapsack. It is easier to strive than to stand,—to work than to wait. But "the love of Christ" has a magic which other motives lack, so to gird the heart that it can pace unswervingly the lonely sentinel beat of duty—and when freighted with life's mysteries, to suffer and be strong.

We have counted the martyr age back into the distant past. We cast a wistful look toward "the brave days of old." Many a generation has ended its march since Polycarp sealed his allegiance in syllables of flame. Sun after sun has set since Latimer and Ridley kindled in the old Smithfield market that candle which, by the grace of God, never shall go out. But all martyrs do not burn at the stake. Every age and clime furnishes recruits for that noble army which is the body-guard of our King. Heroes of the faith live in every hamlet. Bearers of the Cross of Jesus pass us daily on the streets. On the martyr-rolls of heaven are names that are written in our visiting lists. In these homes about us—in these pews beside us— there is many a follower of the Christ, whose life is a long, weary, triumphant martyrdom. The world has left behind it—rack and fagot, but the tongue has lost none of its edge, nor speech its venom, since the long-ago day when David wrote of those "who whet their tongues like a sword, and made ready their arrows even bitter words,"—and many a loyal-hearted follower of Jesus is standing in his lot, a lonely but un-flinching target for the rattling and rankling volleys of the world's contempt. The Gethsemane prayer for submission is hourly winging its way heavenward from hearts that can break, but can never desert. Crowned with thorns and clad in garments of heaviness—many a soul endures in suffering silence, pangs that cannot be measured by physical anguish.

To-morrow morning many a soul
will shoulder the load of its daily life
with a spirit no less heroic than that
with which men used to go to the
stake, yea, with the same unquestion-
ing trustfulness with which the Son
of God went tottering up Golgotha.
Have you never seen a Christian
in loneliness and weariness, stagger-
ing, stumbling, struggling on, broken
in heart, bruised in spirit, but the
brow all aglow with the radiance of a
martyr crown ? Have you never seen
a Christian when nerve was tingling
and flesh quivering in the rude
clutch of disease, dispelling the
shadows of the sick-room by the un-
dimmed fortitude of the martyr
spirit ? Have you never seen the

face of the dying Christian, in that hour when heart and flesh were failing, light up with rapture as through the gathering gloom he beheld a vision of angels? The spirit of worldliness may, in this latter day, have intruded within the hallowed precincts of the sanctuary. It has never extruded the spirit of Christ. Spiritual vigor may, perhaps, lie latent, awaiting the trumpet call that shall summon it to resurrection. It is not dead. It only sleepeth. If occasion should demand it, there are those on the roll of every congregation who, rather than prove false to the Lord that loved them, would plant their feet in the footprints of blood and fire where our fathers stood, crying as they take their stand, " The love of Christ constraineth us."

The supreme and present-day need of the Church is to feel afresh the thrill of this mighty love. The vineyard of the Lord needs to be sown again with this seed of fire. This is an incandescent age. This is an era of burning enthusiasms. In commerce and in art, in culture and in pleasure, men are enthusiasts. There is need of a kindred enthusiasm in religion. The times demand men of athletic piety, men of sinewy faith, men who have a vertebrate Christianity ; who can resist the shock of skeptic assault, who can throw off the malaria of popular doubt, who can stem the current of popular contempt; men who have an intense and an intelligent enthusiasm for the honor of their blessed Lord. If the Church of Christ was set free from the thraldom of earth-born ambitions, from the clash and jar of party jealousies and petty contentions, and was tingling in every fibre with a passion of love for Jesus,—glowing from core to circumference with consuming desire for the honor of His name,—who can tell with what resistless swing the battle-line would sweep the field, and the trumpets peal that triumphant and longed-for hour when "the war-drum beats no longer, and the battle-flags are furled." Who can say what tides of influence would begin to set toward this thrilling consummation if each life in this congregation became the exponent of a single-hearted and whole-souled affection for the Christ of Calvary? Would that it might be so! Would that the Spirit of the living God might come in power; come as a rushing, mighty wind and fan the flame of love for Jesus in the hearts where it now burns low; come as a heavenly fire and kindle with holy ardors the hearts that now are dark and cold; come as a divine Teacher, and make every one of us to feel to the depth of our consciousness that sublimest truth that created intelligence can ever compass, "Jesus, the Son of

God, loved me, and died to save my soul." Let that fact fasten its hold upon the heart, and life will become a boon, fraught with glorious possibilities. Work will become sweet. The future will become bright. All cloud will vanish. Every star will shine. For head and hand and heart will be energized with that same triumphant and holy enthusiasm that beat within the breast of that man of Tarsus, the throb of whose mighty heart we feel across nineteen centuries, as we repeat his words, "The love of Christ constraineth us."

34